DOGS SET VIII

WELSH CORGIS

Jill C. Wheeler
ABDO Publishing Company

visit us at
www.abdopublishing.com

Published by ABDO Publishing Company, 8000 West 78th Street, Edina, Minnesota 55439.
Copyright © 2010 by Abdo Consulting Group, Inc. International copyrights reserved in
all countries. No part of this book may be reproduced in any form without written
permission from the publisher. The Checkerboard Library™ is a trademark and logo of
ABDO Publishing Company.

Printed in the United States of America, North Mankato, Minnesota.
092009
012010

 PRINTED ON RECYCLED PAPER

Cover Photo: Corbis
Interior Photos: Alamy pp. 5, 11, 12, 17; AP Images pp. 9, 10; Corbis pp. 7, 13;
    iStockphoto p. 6; Peter Arnold pp. 15, 19, 21

Series Coordinator: Tamara L. Britton
Editors: Tamara L. Britton, BreAnn Rumsch
Art Direction: Neil Klinepier

Library of Congress Cataloging-in-Publication Data

Wheeler, Jill C., 1964-
 Welsh corgis / Jill C. Wheeler.
    p. cm. -- (Dogs)
 Includes index.
 ISBN 978-1-60453-786-4
 1. Cardigan Welsh corgi--Juvenile literature. 2. Pembroke Welsh corgi--Juvenile
literature. I. Title.
 SF429.C34W47 2010
 636.737--dc22

                                        2009033001

CONTENTS

THE DOG FAMILY

Americans own nearly 75 million dogs. All of these dogs are members of the **Canidae** family. The name comes from the Latin word for "dog," which is *canis*. This family also includes wolves, foxes, and coyotes.

Most scientists believe all modern dogs descend from the gray wolf. Like early humans, wolves were hunters. Humans adopted wolf pups to help them hunt.

About 10,000 years ago, humans began changing from roaming hunters to settled farmers. So, they began **breeding** dogs for different uses. The Welsh corgi was bred to drive farm animals such as cattle, sheep, and geese.

Welsh corgis

WELSH CORGIS

Welsh corgis come from Wales in the United Kingdom. The Pembroke Welsh corgi is from Pembrokeshire. The Cardigan Welsh corgi is from Cardiganshire.

Pembroke corgi roots go back to the year 1107. At that time, Flemish weavers brought schipperke and Pomeranian dogs to Wales. Their descendants developed into the Pembroke corgi. These corgis are also related to the keeshond and spitz **breeds**.

The Cardigan corgi breed is older than the Pembroke. Cardigan corgi ancestors came to Wales from central Europe.

A Pembroke Welsh corgi

They arrived in 1200 BC with the Celts. Cardigan corgis are related to the dachshund. Though the Cardigan is the older **breed**, there are more Pembroke corgis.

Originally, both corgis were considered one breed. It was officially recognized by the **American Kennel Club (AKC)** in 1934. That same year, the English Kennel Club declared the two corgis to be separate breeds. The AKC followed in 1935.

A Cardigan Welsh corgi

WHAT THEY'RE LIKE

Welsh corgis are loving, protective, alert, smart, and easily trained. They make wonderful family companions. They are full of fun and want to be involved in family activities.

The corgi **breeds** were created to work on farms. Many early farmers had flocks of geese or chickens that wandered freely. Corgis were trained to herd these birds. They also rid the farm of rats and other unwanted creatures.

Corgis skillfully drove cattle and pigs to and from the farmyard. Corgis could drive animals much larger than themselves. They did so by nipping at the heels of the herd. The corgi's short height made it easy for the dog to avoid being kicked.

The corgi's friendly personality makes it an excellent
service dog. This Cardigan corgi helps kids learn to read.

COAT AND COLOR

Corgis have a weather-resistant double coat. A long, rough topcoat covers a shorter, soft undercoat. The undercoat acts as **insulation**. This keeps corgis comfortable in all kinds of weather.

Corgi coats do shed. This is most noticeable in spring and summer. At these times, warmer temperatures cause the dogs to shed their undercoats. Frequent brushing can help corgis through this process.

A Pembroke corgi with a black and tan coat

10

Pembroke corgis have a wide variety of coat colors. These include red, dark brown, black and tan, yellow brown, black and white, and blue. Cardigan corgis can be red, sable, **brindle**, black, and blue merle.

It is common for corgis to have white markings. White is most commonly found on the neck, the chest, and the legs. It is also often on the **muzzle** and the tip of the tail.

A Cardigan corgi with a blue merle coat

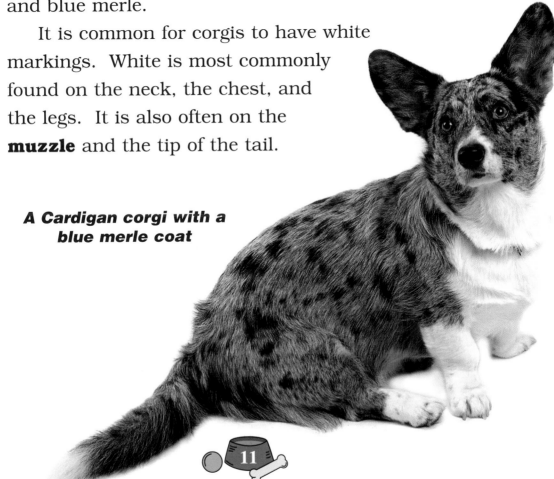

SIZE

Corgis are small, sturdy dogs. Pembroke corgis stand from 10 to 12 inches (25 to 30 cm) tall at the shoulders. Cardigan corgis are about one-half inch (1 cm) taller. This is the same for both males and females.

The similarities stop there, however. Pembroke males weigh about 30 pounds (14 kg) when full grown. Females weigh about 28 pounds (12 kg).

Can you pick out the Cardigan corgi? Do you recognize the Pembroke?

Meanwhile, Cardigan males weigh 30 to 38 pounds (14 to 17 kg). Females weigh an average of 25 to 34 pounds (11 to 15 kg).

The two **breeds** also look different. Cardigan corgis have a long tail. Their ears are big with round tips. Their front legs are slightly bowed, so their toes point outward. Cardigan corgis are longer than Pembroke corgis.

Pembroke corgis have no tail. They have smaller, more pointed ears. Pembrokes also have straight front legs.

CARE

All dogs need regular exercise. The corgi is no exception! Corgis do well in dog sports such as **agility**, herding, and obedience.

It is important to keep a corgi's teeth clean and its nails trimmed. Some **breeders** recommend brushing teeth every day and trimming nails every week. Checking the corgi's eyes, ears, and feet is also important. A good time to do this is while grooming the coat.

All dogs need regular visits to the veterinarian for checkups. The veterinarian will give them **vaccines** against common diseases. He or she can also **spay** or **neuter** corgis.

Corgis can develop several health problems. Both breeds can experience problems with their

joints. And, Pembroke corgis can develop **cancer** and eye problems. The veterinarian will watch for these concerns and work to keep the dog healthy.

The quick, agile corgi is a natural for dog sports such as agility trials.

FEEDING

Each dog has its own dietary needs. These depend on several factors such as age, size, and level of exercise. A veterinarian can suggest a diet based on a dog's needs.

Corgi owners should provide their dogs with a healthy diet. Puppies need several small meals a day. Older dogs can eat one meal each day. All corgis need plenty of fresh water.

It is easy for corgis to gain weight. However, heavy corgis are not as healthy as they should be. Many have a shorter life span. So, owners should carefully watch the amount of food their dogs eat. This will make for healthy, happy corgis.

The name corgi is probably from two Welsh words combined. Cor means "dwarf" and ci means "dog."

THINGS THEY NEED

Corgis need moderate exercise every day. So, owners must make time for their dogs. Daily walks are important.

Owners should also play with their corgis. Toys can help provide exercise, too. Popular toys include hard rubber bones, balls, and rubber rings.

Every corgi needs a collar with license and identification tags. A crate can help with house-training as well as make traveling easier. It also offers the corgi a quiet place to rest. Large, sturdy food and water dishes are a must.

Corgis are affectionate dogs.

These material things are important. But most of all, a dog needs a loving family, **socialization**, and training. This will result in a well-behaved adult dog.

PUPPIES

Corgi mothers are **pregnant** for about 63 days. There are usually five to eight puppies in a **litter**. The puppies are born blind and deaf. They can see and hear after two weeks. One week later, they begin taking their first steps.

If a Welsh corgi is the right dog for you, find a reputable **breeder**. When choosing a puppy, look for one that is active and alert. It should also have an appealing personality. At eight to twelve weeks, a corgi is ready to move to a loving home.

Corgis can begin basic obedience training as soon as they are settled into their new home. Corgis are likely to grow closer to their owners as they train together. A well cared for corgi will be a loving family companion for 12 to 15 years.

When choosing a puppy, pick it up by placing one hand under the chest behind its front legs. Use the other hand to support its rear end.

GLOSSARY

agility - a sport in which a handler leads a dog through an obstacle course during a timed race.

American Kennel Club (AKC) - an organization that studies and promotes interest in purebred dogs.

breed - a group of animals sharing the same ancestors and appearance. A breeder is a person who raises animals. Raising animals is often called breeding them.

brindle - having dark streaks or spots on a gray, tan, or tawny background.

cancer - any of a group of often deadly diseases marked by harmful changes in the normal growth of cells. Cancer can spread and destroy healthy tissues and organs.

Canidae (KAN-uh-dee) - the scientific Latin name for the dog family. Members of this family are called canids. They include domestic dogs, wolves, jackals, foxes, and coyotes.

insulation - material used to keep something from losing or transferring electricity, heat, or sound.

22

litter - all of the puppies born at one time to a mother dog.

muzzle - an animal's nose and jaws.

neuter (NOO-tuhr) - to remove a male animal's reproductive organs.

pregnant - having one or more babies growing within the body.

socialize - to accustom an animal or a person to spending time with others.

spay - to remove a female animal's reproductive organs.

vaccine (vak-SEEN) - a shot given to animals or humans to prevent them from getting an illness or a disease.

WEB SITES

To learn more about Welsh corgis, visit ABDO Publishing Company on the World Wide Web at **www.abdopublishing.com**. Web sites about Welsh corgis are featured on our Book Links page. These links are routinely monitored and updated to provide the most current information available.

INDEX

A
American Kennel Club 7

B
breeder 14, 20

C
Canidae (family) 4
character 8, 16, 19, 20
chest 11
coat 10, 11, 14
collar 18
color 11
crate 18

E
ears 13, 14
English Kennel Club 7
exercise 14, 16, 18
eyes 14, 15

F
feet 14
food 16, 18

G
grooming 10, 14

H
health 14, 15, 16
history 4, 6, 7, 8

L
legs 11, 13
license 18
life span 16, 20

M
muzzle 11

N
nails 14
neck 11
neuter 14

P
puppies 16, 20

R
reproduction 20

S
shedding 10
shoulders 12
size 8, 12, 13, 16
spay 14

T
tail 11, 13
teeth 14
toys 18
training 8, 18, 19, 20

V
vaccines 14
veterinarian 14, 15, 16

W
Wales 6
water 16, 18
work 4, 8